Praise for DECIDE

"As a global business leader, Augie Fabela has faced many crises requiring high-stakes decisions and consequences. Applying his DECIDE framework in law enforcement tactical operations is a fresh, structured way to help ensure mission success."

–Sheriff Thomas J. Dart
Cook County Sheriff (Chicago)

"Peace officers represent the thin blue line between a safe, ordered society and the unthinkable alternative. DECIDE provides great insight into how law enforcement can make the best decision when the pressure is on. A compelling read that has practical utility beyond its intended audience of police officers."

–Allan D. Cors
President of the National Rifle Association

"Augie Fabela has bridged the divergent worlds of global business with his extensive training and background in law enforcement to offer a practical and thought-provoking approach to crisis management and tactical decision making in the twenty-first century."

–Chairman Edward M. Burke
City of Chicago Council Alderman Finance Chairman
Former Chicago Police Officer

"Today's law enforcement confronts unprecedented circumstances. We require out-of-the-box thinking and tactics. DECIDE presents the progressive measures necessary to get the mission accomplished. Augie has dedicated his talent, time, and heart to improving law enforcement decision making."

–Chief Joel H. Brumlik
Winthrop Harbor Police Department

"In law enforcement, the concept of thinking globally yet acting locally has never been more practically applied—until now! The DECIDE model clearly demonstrates the inter-relationship between lessons learned in the global business arena and how they can be applied simply and successfully to solve today's critical law enforcement challenges."

–Sheriff Kevin Rambosk
Collier County Sheriff

D|E|C|I|D|E

All proceeds from this book will be donated to support law enforcement training and safety.

DECIDE

TACTICAL CRISIS DECISION MAKING

A FRAMEWORK FOR LAW ENFORCEMENT

CHIEF AUGIE K FABELA II

COOK COUNTY SHERIFF'S OFFICE-CHICAGO

CO-FOUNDER OF A GLOBAL MULTI-BILLION DOLLAR COMPANY

Printed in the United States of America

Library of Congress Control Number: 2017954262

ISBN Paperback: 978-1-947368-19-4
ISBN eBook: 978-1-947368-20-0

Book Cover Design: Peter Arnell
Interior Design: Ghislain Viau

*To the visionary leaders and committed men and
women of law enforcement: our everyday heroes who put
their lives and well-being on the line to protect and serve
our communities. It is an honor and privilege to have joined
the ranks of over a million brothers and sisters in blue.*

Contents

SECTION THREE
The Tactical DECIDE Model

Preface

LAW ENFORCEMENT IS UNDER SIEGE TODAY AS never before. We are in the crosshairs of not only killers who have specifically targeted sworn officers, but also of society itself, which second-guesses the decisions its members have paid law enforcement officers to make.

The fundamental elements of the DECIDE model focus on decision making and judgment training. This training should have the same priority as firearms, hand-to-hand combat and arrest tactics. As recent incidents have been highly publicized, there is a growing misunderstanding that law enforcement generally reacts without measured and well-thought-out judgment, process, and training. This is not reality!

Compounding the difficulty of the current situation is the fact that there are always two sides to every situation, and we can only do our best to train our side of it, in this case, law enforcement. The other side will always be a variable. It is important to note that regardless of how much training you do receive, sometimes the situation is not going to go as planned or have the desired outcome. Things can go poorly when you are trying to deal with an uncontrollable subject or situation. The reality is that these can be life-threatening situations and you must do the best you can under the circumstances that you are facing.

It is equally important to note, however, that strategic decision making and judgment are trainable skill sets. An increase in training in these areas will better serve the public and the law enforcement community. While this training is not the panacea that is going solve everything, I hope it will be a valuable tool for law enforcement.

For a few years, I have hesitated to write this book and make the connection between global business leadership and law enforcement tactical crisis decision making strategies. I prepared the DECIDE model for law enforcement years ago, but only shared it with a tight circle of law enforcement tactical commanders and team leaders. I am a businessperson and entrepreneur who decided to dedicate part of my life to serving as a sworn police officer in the State of Illinois. The skills I learned in business have proven successful in the world of law enforcement (and some of the skills I have learned in law enforcement have made me a more effective businessperson—but that is not a subject for this book). The seemingly impossible challenges facing my fellow officers have compelled me to share these proven decision making strategies.

In this short book, you will find a tried and tested method for crisis decision making unlike anything you have encountered in your training or your law enforcement career. The ideas underlying the DECIDE model come from my experience starting a telecom business in Russia during the fall of the Soviet Union—a tense era of political change and chaos for the Russian people—and the subsequent challenge of growing that company in many very challenging countries around the world.

The DECIDE model worked in Moscow. It worked in Algeria. It worked in Chicago. And I am confident that it will work for you.

I do not want this book to come across as merely an attempt to promote my business accomplishments. I could never have built VEON without the help of God and the cadre of excellent leaders and professionals I have been fortunate enough to work with over the last twenty-five years. Without them, the company would never have grown from thirteen employees to over sixty thousand, to become the seventh-largest mobile communications firm in the world, with over 235 million subscribers (more than AT&T

and Verizon). I do not pretend to be a management and decision making guru. Equally important, I want to make it clear that I do not believe I am a law enforcement expert either. I remain a student for life, always seeking to learn new things and new skills.

What I do know and what I have learned—through direct experience—is how to take advantage of opportunities. That is, how to lead and navigate adversity and crises involving multiple stakeholders with different views and objectives, with high-stakes consequences for success and failure.

My audience for this book, by training, nature, and experience, is made up of very skeptical individuals: cops. I hope the DECIDE model withstands the scrutiny of police officers, tactical commanders, team leaders, and law enforcement command staff in terms of credibility and engagement. I purposefully designed this book to be a fast read—one that can be consumed in a single sitting of under two hours—as I suspect my target audience is very much like me: impatient and unwilling to stay seated for any length of time, always anxious to take action.

My vision for this book is to promote the importance and effectiveness of learning and training leadership and tactical crisis decision making skills in law enforcement. I hope by the time you finish reading this short book, and are running your teams through scenario-based tactical crisis decision making exercises, you will join me in appreciating and evangelizing the need to train leadership and decision making in your agency or department.

Train to DECIDE
Decide to train!

NASDAQ 100 Listing. $45 Billion Peak Valuation.

VEON: World's 7th Largest Mobile Enterprise, 235 Million Customers, More than AT&T and Verizon: Covering 10% of the Global Population.

Davos World Economic Forum Chairmen Community Founding Member.

Since 2000 Actively Contributing to "Improving the State of the World".

Who Is Augie K Fabela II?

Founding and Running a Business Amid the Havoc of Post-Soviet Russia

TWENTY-FIVE YEARS AGO, IN THE EARLY '90S, I embarked on a great business adventure: founding a Telecom company in Moscow. We started VEON with thirteen employees and grew it into a global company with more than sixty thousand employees, covering 10 percent of the world's population, with revenues of over $20 billion in 2014. We became the seventh-largest mobile Telecom company in the world, with more than 235 million subscribers. VEON rose into the NASDAQ 100 Index—meaning, it ranked as one of the top 100 NASDAQ-listed companies—and in 1996, it became the first Russian company ever to list on the New York Stock Exchange. It has been a whirlwind journey from

From Moscow, Soviet Union in 1991 to the World's Financial Capital, NYC in 1996.

Making History: First Russian and Telecom Company to IPO on NYSE.

Moscow, the birthplace of Soviet Communism, to New York, the global center of capitalism.

When I started VEON, I was only twenty-five years old, and had a very limited business background. I had not gone to business school and I had no significant corporate experience. Fresh out of Stanford University, with an undergraduate degree in international relations and a graduate master's degree in international policy, I spent two years working in Japan for the country's largest mass-media group. I learned a lot about Japanese business and did my work in Japanese, but that was a far cry from what I would be exposed to just two years later in the Soviet Union.

I was a young entrepreneur—armed only with a vision, passion, and unshakable optimism—seeking opportunity in Moscow, which was then still part of the Soviet Union; the Berlin Wall had not yet fallen. By the time I went to Russia, not only had I worked in a Japanese mega-company in Tokyo, I had also started three companies in the United States: one in the marketing sector, one in the IT-services sector, and one in the service sector. I had worked with AT&T Bell Labs, Amoco Oil, and Northrop Grumman, providing IT contract services and solutions. In 1990, I had also ventured into the craze of employee-leasing companies, which specialized in creating a flexible workforce through outsourcing (before outsourcing meant sending work overseas).

At age twenty-five, I had already had a wide variety of experiences. But none of those experiences prepared me for what I would face in Russia. We formally founded VEON in 1992. I signed my first joint-venture agreement (*Protocol* in Russian) in 1991 under Soviet law. In those days, Russia was being turned upside down. Capitalism was brand-new and the government was in upheaval. As I soon found out, I was not the only one looking for opportunity.

> At age twenty-five, I had already had a wide variety of experiences. But none of those experiences prepared me for what I would face in Russia.

The crises started off small. Just operating a business in Russia was a huge challenge because the people I was working with were not businesspeople. They had *no* experience in business because there had been no such thing as private businesses in Soviet Russia. Working and making decisions with people who just did not understand the basic principles of business and capitalism was definitely a challenge. They did not even understand simple concepts like marketing or customer service, let alone what the more complicated concept of conflict of interest meant; it just was not part of their lives or job experience.

They also did not understand the concepts of corporate share ownership or joint ventures: I put in cash and in-kind equipment contributions, they put in their services and know-how, and we would share fifty-fifty in the venture. It sounds like a simple, very obvious thing to agree upon, but my partner would say, "Well, I brought in these additional new things, so I want more shares now." They could not understand that capitalism just did not work that way. It was tough to manage a partner who had a completely different frame of reference for how ownership, decision making, and management structures all worked, and who did not understand that putting licenses and permits under his own company name—instead of the name of the joint-venture company—was a conflict of interest and wrong.

These were the earliest challenges I faced—but it was not long before they grew into much bigger ones. Many arose simply from the fact that in those early days, we were a cash business. Hardly anybody in Russia had bank accounts, so we sold our phones—which we priced at US$5,000—*for cold, hard cash*. I recall the demand was so high that even though I tried to limit the number of subscribers to only one thousand to ensure that we did not overload the network and deteriorate the quality of service, we quickly had a waiting list of customers in the thousands, and our salespeople were receiving offers of US$1,000 to be moved to the top of the waiting list to get a mobile phone.

In hindsight, it should have been obvious that a cash business would attract attention from the *wrong* people. I found this out the hard way about two and a half years into the development of the company. We had set up a marketing and distribution office, out of which we handled our commercial operations. My right-hand man, my First Vice President, was a Russian ex-military guy who looked straight out of the movies: hard core, strong, did not talk much; you get the picture. He would just look at you and you would instantly be terrified to cross his path. I was happy to have him on my side, even though he thought I was just a foolish American *boy*.

> In hindsight, it should have been obvious that a cash business would attract attention from the *wrong* people.

One gray-winter late morning, we were in our offices when five men entered. They were huge, intimidating guys wearing heavy coats. I remember noticing they had scars on their faces, necks, and hands. They proceeded to tell us that we were in *their* territory, and that there was a fee to be paid if we wanted to continue to operate. If we paid the fee, they would protect us from all the *hooligans* in the territory, so we had better comply. They told us they would be back to start collecting the payment, and then, in a very organized, impressive, and purposeful manner, they exited the building, all moving off in different directions, completely coordinated—just like in the movies when a band of sophisticated bank robbers quickly blend into a crowd and the surrounding environment.

Being the confident, young, naïve entrepreneur that I was, I remained quite calm. They had spoken mostly in Russian, which I did not speak, but I had gathered this was a shakedown and that they wanted money from us. *Well, I* thought, *we're not going to give it to them, so we'll just have to figure something out.* Then I looked over to my right-hand man—this stalwart, stoic, don't-mess-with-me guy—and he was literally shaking. His hands were shaking and his voice was trembling; he was terrified. That was when I realized I should probably be concerned too, if not for me, then most definitely for him and our office staff.

As the supposed consummate problem solver, I knew immediately what to do . . . or so I'd thought. I had already engaged a group that was helping me figure out how to safely and effectively operate a consumer-facing business in the early days of Russian capitalism. This group had offered their help to me and I had thought, *Great, aren't these nice people!* I'd felt fortunate—and even smart—to have found them. All I had to do was pay them a reasonable and normal sales commission for the work they were helping us with, no upfront fees or costs. In my mind, at the time, I had everything dialed in brilliantly with this group.

So after this encounter, I went to the leaders of this group and told them of our troubles. They were extraordinarily calm and professional, and more than happy to offer their services to help with this "very Russian problem," as they called it. "Don't worry about it," they told me. "We'll take care of them." There was just one catch: "But in return, you have to give us exclusivity for distribution in all of Moscow."

In hindsight it seems quite possible that the whole thing was staged; that this group had sent those five guys in order to push us toward them. I will never know. As far as I could tell from my experience to that point, they seemed to be good commercial businessmen who had been delivering proven results for us. They were all very sophisticated and looked completely normal. It had seemed reasonable enough to accept their services. But now it was quite clear that they really had no intention of being reasonable at all.

When I told them we could not possibly give them exclusive distribution, their true faces started to show. After it became clear that we had no intention of meeting these demands, the threats started—from different (but similarly professional and clean-cut) representatives of the same group. The threats were phrased as warnings about my professional career, but they were made in person, and the body language was crystal clear: "do it or die." I was not the most astute Russophile, but I did follow

The threats were phrased as warnings about my professional career, but they were made in person, and the body language was crystal clear: "do it or die."

the local news enough to know that every week some executive was assassinated or beaten on the streets of Moscow. For the first few times they pressed me, I just smiled and changed the subject to more pleasant things. However, the threats continued to escalate over the next few weeks and it finally reached the point where I actually had to flee my apartment in the middle of the night, escorted by a security detail that my (now more composed) right-hand man had organized for me. It was so bad that I had to temporarily leave the country due to the death threats.

Thankfully, our partner had come out of the military, and he had recruited other talented engineers from the military. Our company was unique in that regard. We were offering something that nobody else could offer: the opportunity for military engineers to convert over to the commercial world. Very few companies in the early '90s were brave enough to be working in post-Soviet Russia, and even fewer were inclined to recruit from the military ranks. Therefore, we stood out as being good for the development of Russia. As a result, we had a lot of goodwill in Moscow—especially within the military community—and we were able to organize allies in the community to support us.

The goodwill we enjoyed from the government and the old military industrial complex was a significant strength. In the end, we settled things with the group because it became clear to them from many voices in Moscow that the threats and intimidation should stop.

When you are young, you make many decisions without really knowing exactly what you are doing. To be fair, these were situations that, as an American, I was not accustomed to dealing with at all. These people were so smooth in their talk and actions. At a very young age, I was encountering situations you would think only happen in the movies. I never thought I would be forced to make decisions that could affect the lives of my friends and employees—not to mention my own life!

Through all of this, even when threats forced me to flee the country for a few months, I never worried about my safety. Fear never really registered. Firstly, it was because I was naïve and optimistic. Secondly, it was because I was extraordinarily confident that I had a purpose in being in Russia, and I knew that God had my point, my six, and my flanks covered. And like any good entrepreneur, I was not going to give up, no matter what!

This was not the only problem we faced as we grew the company either. There were high-stakes decisions to be made about ownership of shares, distribution territories, client accounts, and collections. Three times over, our shares and ownership in the company disappeared. It sounds impossible, but this was Russia in the 1990s. We literally had to re-buy our ownership back three times. It was, of course, discouraging, but I just could not accept failure; I was not going to let anything or anyone stand in the way of my mission! Of course, VEON started with a massive vision, but a very small bank account.

> Three times over, our shares and ownership in the company disappeared. It sounds impossible, but this was Russia in the 1990s.

The initial money for our first investment I literally had to fund with credit card cash advances, using lots of credit cards. We simply had to find new and better ways to ensure that we could keep the company together and not lose all the time, effort, and money we had put into it. Frankly, it was not so much about losing what we had invested; it was more about having a clear vision of what the potential was and not accepting having to walk away from that.

As we expanded VEON, we had to overcome everything from economic and political crises to specific regulatory issues and cultural problems. We faced circumstances that I was not used to dealing with, many of which were far from business as usual. There was no book or Google to research how to deal with these types of extreme adversities.

These experiences were incredibly formative, requiring great presence of mind and strong tactical decision making at every step of the journey. People wanted to take my life; they wanted to take my company; they wanted to take everything I had. These events formed a fundamental basis for how I think and operate: I am always optimistic, I continually work to resolve issues, and I never lose sight of the final objective. Through it all, however, I never could have imagined that the challenge of founding and building a business in Russia and globally would prepare me for the next chapter of my life: law enforcement.

> I am always optimistic, I continually work to resolve issues, and I never lose sight of the final objective.

Entering the World of Law Enforcement

In 2009 I was asked to use my management experience to help a 501(c)3 not-for-profit organization called Air-One Emergency Response Coalition, a search-and-rescue helicopter unit. Air-One was privately funded, but it supported police and fire departments, assisting with searches for lost children and Alzheimer's patients (especially in the cold Chicago winters), in addition to providing a range of other emergency services. Air-One was the brainchild of three idealistic individuals in Illinois: a brilliant pilot with a mission, a visionary Police Chief who believed he could really make a difference, and a philanthropic patron with a helicopter.

I was introduced to Air-One by one of the members of the organization's board of directors, a prominent Chicago Alderman and former Chicago police officer. The organization was struggling financially—their coffers were empty and they literally could not afford the fuel to fly any missions—so I made a small contribution to help temporarily pay for fuel.

However, in order to survive, AirOne needed to be reorganized so it could have a steady funding source and a structure that would allow it to operate on its own, rather than relying on just a few people to donate money for fuel. It needed a healthy, sustainable business model to continue its missions of search-and-rescue, tactical aerial support for law enforcement, and public safety.

With my involvement, we were able to refocus the Air-One command staff and professionally reorganize and restructure the organization. We expanded the mission of the organization to include Homeland Security emergency preparedness, training for disaster recovery, emergency logistics, and tactical operations team deployments and extractions. With this new mission we were able to form relationships with several Homeland Security agencies and task forces to obtain training grants for Air-One.

In addition to our new mission, we were also able to strengthen our relationship with the U.S. Department of Defense, which enabled us to acquire more surplus helicopters to grow our fleet. Air-One had a fleet of eight helicopters—more than any other public agency in all of Illinois, likely making it the largest volunteer search-and-rescue air unit in the entire United States.

Every member of Air-One was a police officer or a firefighter, or had some connection to law enforcement or public safety. So, in recognition of my involvement and as a way to keep me involved in Air-One, I was offered the opportunity to be sworn in as a police officer. I was very appreciative, and it was certainly cool. What guy would not find it cool to have a police badge? If I were to have a badge, however, I wanted to be like any other cop. I did not want any shortcuts, and I did not want any special favors. So I said,

> If I were to have a badge, however, I wanted to be like any other cop. I did not want any shortcuts, and I did not want any special favors.

"I'll accept being sworn in, but I want to do it like every other cop. I want to go to the Police Academy." The Chief of Winthrop Harbor Police Department said he would not have it any other way! He swore me in and ordered me to the Police Academy as a cadet.

The first step was passing the required physical-fitness test. I was in my forties and all the other cadets were in their twenties. Naturally, I had to prove to myself that I could outdo them and finish ahead of them in all the physical tests. And after training for four months, I indeed outperformed all the other cadets. I attended the Police Academy for a year and became a certified law enforcement officer in Illinois.

But this was not enough for me, and because I was blessed with control of my schedule and had the resources, I was able to put myself through a huge amount of tactical training. I trained with unit trainers from the U.S. Department of Defense Special Operations Command (SOCOM), Special Forces, and members of USNORTHCOM/NORAD, Delta Force, SEAL Team Six, Chicago SWAT, Illinois Tactical Officers Association, and the FBI Hostage Rescue Team— the most elite SWAT team in the United States.

I was passionate about doing my job as proficiently as possible, and to do that, I needed to train at the best possible level. I was coming late to the game; most law enforcement officers my age already had twenty years of experience under their belts. I wanted to be just as good or better, so I did everything I could to catch up. After all my training, I still wanted to go further. So I went to SWAT school and became a certified SWAT operator, again outperforming my class of twenty five experienced officers in shooting qualifications as a result of all the extensive training I had done.

Because I was associated with a police helicopter unit, I was able to gain direct access to many unique operations. When you are part of an air unit, you provide such a great asset that you instantly become part of the command structure of any operation you are called upon to support. I was therefore able to instantly get exposure to many incidents and learn how law enforcement incident command operated. And in order to better operate within this environment, I got fully certified in the Homeland Security Directives on National Incident Management System (NIMS) and Incident Command System (ICS).

I have continued to dive deeper and deeper into the law enforcement world. Along with my continued involvement with Air-One as Commander of Special Operations, I also now work with the Winthrop Harbor Police Department and the Cook County Sheriff's Office. In Winthrop Harbor, I united and reestablished our SWAT team. Winthrop Harbor had had a SWAT team in the past, but there had been a loss of focus and no training. I restarted the program, and when the Chief asked me to become Commander of Special Operations, I accepted.

From Global Entrepreneur to Police Academy to Police Helicopter Unit Commander.

AIR-ONE Helicopter Unit: Transition from VEON to Law Enforcement.

Cook County, which includes the City of Chicago, is the second largest county in the United States. I was introduced to the Cook County Sheriff when NATO was holding its annual global summit in Chicago. Air-One had air operations on standby to assist, and we were working with the FBI and U.S. Department of Defense USNORTHCOM/NORAD. I was once again at the center of the command structure, where I was able to observe events and advise the Sheriff. I was in no way a tactical guru, but I had experience with program management, risk analysis, decision making, evaluations, and making sure everyone was focusing on the right issues. With this experience, I was able to help keep things organized by communicating what the Sheriff did and did not want the agency to focus on. I also spent most of my time on the streets where the protestors were, which enabled me to keep the Sheriff apprised of street operations and developments in real-time.

After I had helped with the NATO Summit, the Sheriff asked me to join the Sheriff's Office to help reorganize some of the units in there. In doing so, he swore me in as Special Assistant to the Sheriff and I became involved with the Central Warrant Unit, a ninety-person unit with over forty thousand warrants to serve in Chicago and Cook County. I helped reorganize and consolidate the Unit, which was spread across three offices at different physical locations. I restructured the management, policies, and training, and established new headquarters. In keeping with my new role in overseeing the unit, the Sheriff appointed me Commander of Law Enforcement Operations and subsequently promoted me to the rank of Chief.

Being part of this elite unit was extremely valuable in helping me catch up to those who had twenty plus years of experience on me. There is no better way to catch up quickly than by working the South and West sides of Chicago at night, with shots being fired around you as you are serving warrants and arresting people while hostile crowds berate you and try to surround you in an attempt to intimidate you and show support to their fellow gang members who are being arrested. It is an environment that forces you to develop tactical and situational awareness. You have to be tactically sound in order to make sure that you and your team are as safe as possible. You need to plan and make good decisions every night as you assess each case and manage hostile crowds teeming with people carrying concealed weapons.

From my very first exposure to the law enforcement command structure all the way through this on-the-ground field tactical experience, I noticed that the approach to getting things done and making decisions was never as organized or efficient as it could be. Moreover, I observed that the tactical decisions necessary in law enforcement operations were very similar in many ways to the decisions

I was constantly making while leading VEON through its challenges and crises. In both cases, you have to know where you want to end up even though you do not know everything that could happen along the way. In both cases you need to have the presence of mind, focus, the ability to reorient, and the drive to persevere on a mission until you complete it.

As I continue to become more involved in law enforcement, I have come to realize that my experiences over the past twenty years with VEON could help me make a larger institutional contribution by empowering law enforcement officers, supervisors, commanders, and agencies to better succeed in fulfilling their difficult and complex missions. With each mission that I have observed, participated in, or led, it became clear that there was a need for training in leadership and decision making, and that there could be immediate benefits from applying decision making models similar to those I utilized in making my business decisions. In particular, with the extreme challenges I faced in the course of the development of VEON, I came to realize that the high-stress, high-stakes decision making required for a successful law enforcement mission could benefit from the proven tactical decision making model I have used successfully in global business.

Cook County Sheriff Dart Swearing-in. NATO Chicago & Fugitive Warrant Operations.

From AIR-ONE to Winthrop Harbor SWAT to Cook County Sheriff.

Law Enforcement Needs Training in Leadership and Tactical Decision Making

The Connection Between Global Business and Law Enforcement Leadership and Decision Making Tactics

WHEN I ENTERED THE WORLD OF LAW ENFORCEMENT, it did not take me long to notice the strong connection between global business and law enforcement decision making tactics. Building and running a dynamic global business requires constant crisis decision making and leadership; running a tactical unit and executing an operation or mission requires those same qualities from tactical operators. Both environments deal with high-stakes decisions that affect high-value assets and objectives, and vast numbers of people.

Running a business in Russia, we faced a huge range of crises. We had our telecom licenses (the core of our business) under threat of being taken away by the government. In another incident, a competitor attempting to outmaneuver us instigated a US$700 million tax claim against us when our revenues were only US$300 million, which, of course, is crazy—how could our tax liability be twice our revenue? All of this made it pretty clear what the objective was: to annihilate us. During the course of growing the business and dealing with crises, we faced many hard decisions, including leadership decisions, such as whether or not to change our loyal founding top leadership and key contributors when the skills required for those jobs changed with the company's growth and expanded complexity.

One of our competitors was believed to be very *friendly* with the Minister of Telecommunications. This competitor was trying to muscle us out of the market, and in order to do so, they fabricated a regulation that we had supposedly violated. Based on that *violation*, they moved to have our license suspended. By this time we had already accumulated over one million subscribers. If our license had been suspended, we would have had to shut down, putting all those subscribers out of service, and the company would have ceased to exist. We were being forced into a corporate life-or-death situation.

In this situation, negotiation with the regulators was not practical or viable. They were leading the attack against us. We had direct contact with them, but they were never sincere about working things out because they had ulterior motives. We had to find alternate means of dealing with this crisis. The very first thing we did was form a crisis management team (led by a Russian team leader), whose sole purpose was to solve the issue. This team communicated with the Russian PR side, the government side, and the bureaucratic agencies side, while I raised the issues on the U.S. political and investors' side.

One of the key reasons we pushed to go public and list on the New York Stock Exchange, becoming the first Russian company to list equities on the NYSE, was to get U.S. Government support and to have a base of large institutional investors as a countervailing force against any arbitrary actions within Russia. Early post-Soviet Russia was a difficult place to work, and I decided that the best defense would be transparency. The NYSE listing was a tool I used to implement a policy of disclosure.

Through a combination of political, economic, and media pressure, we were able to get the right senior level Russian government officials to intervene and rein in the agencies and ministries that were being manipulated into attacking us for competitive self-interest. The regulation claim was withdrawn and the tax claim turned into a negotiated nominal payment to the Russian government. The whole effort took about nine months from beginning to end and not a single aspect of this crisis could have been managed without the crisis management team we had put in place. Nor could the situation have been resolved without visualizing the end result, which was for senior leadership in the Russian Government to step in to protect foreign investment in Russia. That was an audacious end result for an independent and (at the time) relatively small company to visualize. However, the path to the solution was very clearly defined.

Although the mission objective and general oversight came from the CEO and myself (the Chairman), the crisis team was not directly led by either of us. We put one person in charge of solving this crisis, and that person was assigned to work on all facets of the operation day to day—a war room chief, or "incident commander" in law enforcement ICS speak.

It is important to remember that in crisis management, the chain of command does not necessarily follow rank. In global business, when you face a crisis situation, it is not necessarily the Chairman, CEO, President, or any senior executive making all the decisions. It is not just by virtue of position or title that you are able to make the right decisions. The decisions have to be made by the people who are closest to the problem and who really know and understand it inside and out. Naturally, that person has to have the leadership and technical skills to do the job, and they need to be empowered from the top of the chain of command. They also need to have their "six" covered, so they can focus on looking forward. In corporate speak, that means that upper management needs to protect them from corporate politics.

> It is important to remember that in crisis management, the chain of command does not necessarily follow rank.

Of course we had a chain of command and key decisions were floated up, but we needed to localize the problem solving and decision making. It was vital to have a command structure that was focused, nimble, and close to the information, so the right decisions could be made. We could not have someone parachuting in, pretending that just because he had a title, he could make the right decisions. In this particular example, we were dealing with a specifically Russian issue; how could anyone other than a Russian understand the culture, the language, or the bureaucracy associated with the crisis? It would have been a huge mistake to pretend we could do it any other way.

One of the first things I noticed in the world of law enforcement was a certain degree of disorganization, not due to negligence, but rather, to enthusiasm. In general, many police officers have type-A personalities; they have a passion to solve whatever problem is at hand. In fact, that is their job! That is a great attitude to have when you are patrolling alone in a squad car, and it still works when you are driving with a partner. But when you get fifteen or twenty officers together who all want to be the one to solve the problem, things can easily become inefficient and sometimes even unsafe. I frequently saw situations in which intentions were excellent and individual actions were great, but as a team, there was complete disorganization and even chaos. When you need everyone to act as a team, you need training, a clear field chain of command, and a strong leader who will step up, take control, and make the key decisions.

Training Tactical Crisis Decision Making

The idea of having a system for crisis decision making for law enforcement is not entirely new. After September 11, 2001, the U.S. Federal government mandated the National Incident Management System (NIMS) and the Incident

Command System (ICS). The purpose of NIMS was to ensure that command structures were not necessarily static or rank based, but mission focused. Under these systems, everyone has a more structured role to play in the final mission, rather than just tackling whatever problem he or she saw at hand. In theory, everybody in law enforcement knows NIMS and ICS, but unfortunately, in practice, the system can sometimes fall apart. Especially for tactical operations, there needs to be a simple protocol that can withstand the pressure of a crisis.

The problem comes down to knowledge and training. To be fair, NIMS does try to implement training, but people tend to view it as just one more regulation, general order, or policy out of hundreds. They will abide by it, but they do not take it to heart or understand its value due to its perceived complexity. There is no true decision making training in the law enforcement world, partly because decision making training sounds like such a strange thing.

The truth is, effective decision making training is not only possible, it is essential! In law enforcement, just about everybody understands the importance of training. Everyone understands that you need the *muscle memory*, the ingraining of a motion or action derived from training repetition. Both the law enforcement and military communities know that *under stress you do not perform to the level of your skills; you perform to the level of your training.* People do not realize that the same is true for decision making. Not only is training for decision making absent from the law enforcement world; it is sometimes seen as not important, as not *real* police work. That is just plain wrong.

During one of our trainings, I led a training session for a SWAT team. We did a tabletop training exercise for which we literally sat around a table in a conference room. A Chicago SWAT leader defined the scenario and acted as moderator, putting all kinds of facts on the table as they occurred: a shooter, a hostage, someone coming to the window, shots fired, notifying the chief, organizing the teams, coordinating multiple agencies and departments that showed up to help. We made the team and team leaders react, decide, instruct, delegate, and define their roles and responsibilities and those of others.

These team leaders were people who could lead a team into a building, deal with any situation they might encounter, and clear it. I would have no doubts about their ability to succeed or about the safety of the team. I would have no doubts about their decision making skills in that scenario, or about their ability to make sure the mission was

> Not only is training for decision making absent from the law enforcement world; it is sometimes seen as not important, as not *real* police work.

completed and that the subject facility was secured. But it was amazing to see how these capable leaders and experienced operators quickly became challenged and fell into indecision when they had to deal with seventeen things at once; with a complex chain of command; with a constantly changing crisis; and with multiple stakeholders, multiple constituencies, multiple objectives, and multiple interests. It was fascinating to see how their eyes opened up throughout the training.

When you only have one job to do, it is straightforward to go in and get that job done. But when you have to deal with a whole bunch of things all at once, it is an entirely different story. This is what business leaders do every day; there are always scores of different things to deal with all at once. In law enforcement, there may be many calls over the course of a day, but officers are generally only dealing with one call at a time. In a crisis scenario, it is never just one call at a time, and you cannot afford to be crippled with indecision—even for a second. You need to make constant decisions, you need to delegate wisely, and you need to lead!

How Is Tactical Crisis Decision Making Different from Ordinary Decision Making?

The first and most obvious difference between tactical crisis decision making and ordinary decision making is immediacy and urgency. Once you are called in to deal with a problem, you are in the middle of a crisis that needs resolution, and it is up to you to resolve the problem successfully.

Think about it in the context of a fire. If there is a fire in your home, you need to make very urgent and immediate decisions. You do not sit and wait for the fire department to show up, and you do not convene a group to decide what to do. You take immediate action!

If you are responding to a domestic disturbance, you will approach with caution, engage the subjects, take control of the scene, and at times have to physically restrain and/or arrest one or more subjects. Emotions and tempers can be extremely high, but you follow procedure to diffuse the situation and take control. Although you are making rapid decisions and reacting to emotional escalation, which could lead to a volatile situation, it is still not a full-blown crisis.

In a crisis, there is a greater urgency that does not allow for *business as usual* in your decision making. In addition to the urgency, you are going to be dealing with high-pressure, high-emotions, high-stakes, and severe consequences for errors. Whether those high-stakes are

> In a crisis, there is a greater urgency that does not allow for *business as usual* in your decision making.

related to finances or property, or whether they are literally life and death, they increase the need for focus and discipline.

Crises are inherently complex. There are almost always many different actors involved in a law enforcement context. There are the perpetrators and victims, the command staff and officers/operators, the innocent bystanders and media (with smart phones, everyone is a reporter), the various agencies and emergency services, and the general public, who will be scrutinizing your actions as the situation unfolds, as well as in its aftermath. In most, if not all cases, all of these constituencies will have different objectives, roles, and responsibilities, and by virtue of their different roles and responsibilities, they will all have different and often conflicting organizational and personal agendas.

Because of this, consensus decision making in a crisis situation will never succeed. As a leader, you have to keep the focus on the final objective; you need to visualize the desired end result. This can be difficult, because in a crisis situation, everybody wants to contribute to the solution, react immediately, resolve the problem at hand, and be a hero. This is all well and good, but it is impossible to act quickly and efficiently when everybody is trying to act independently. This causes conflict and chaos. One person has to be the leader; you need a single incident commander at the very beginning of the crisis.

It is important to note that the foregoing is not an endorsement for an overly authoritarian approach to decision making. Consultation, advice, and experience all play a role—but managing the decision making process in a high-stakes, high-stress situation requires skill.

So how do you find that balance when you have twelve different people with twelve different opinions all wanting to save the day? As a leader, you need to quickly evaluate the strengths and weaknesses of the team as a whole. Based on that, you can add weight to the judgment of different people on the basis of their individual strengths, weaknesses, experience, and motivations. It is important to remember to take people's motives into account, because they may be offering advice based not on their experience, but, rather, on their own organizational or personal agendas.

When you have a lot of different opinions, you have to take what you can to define the appropriate final objective and formulate the right plan. Then you have to form an execution team to put the plan into action. At the end of the day, there has to be one person making the decisions, and you have

> When you have a lot of different opinions, you have to take what you can to define the appropriate final objective and formulate the right plan.

to delegate roles and responsibilities as best you can in the time you have.

While tactical crisis decision making does not lend itself to consensual decision making, the more input you get in the planning stage, the better your plan will be. However, although the plan can and should be devised with the involvement of a wider group and leadership, once you enter the execution phase, there can only be one leader: one decision maker leading the execution of the plan.

There has to be a clear and defined final objective—one plan, one mode of execution—and everybody must get on board, regardless of his or her own personal feelings or agendas. If someone keeps contradicting you and is not on board with the final plan and objective, you have to remove that individual because he or she will affect the confidence and effectiveness of the team.

As the leader and decision maker, everyone will be looking to you to resolve the crisis. You will bear the blame or you will receive the credit—although in reality, you must be prepared to receive credit only from your immediate team, which should be sufficient anyway. In most cases, and especially in a large crisis, there are plenty of people of rank who will quickly step in to take the credit. As a leader and tactical crisis decision maker, you need to focus on your mission and know that it is your decisions that will result either in you and your team achieving zero, or you and your team being heroes.

The Five Key Principles of Successful Crisis Decision Making by a Leader

Whether you are making key business decisions or key tactical operations execution decisions, there are five key principals for successful high-stress decision making by a leader. No matter what kind of crisis or decision you are facing, a good leader will always, in some way, adhere to these five principles:

1. Know how to judge and balance the who, what, when, how, and why.

Every decision point can lead you down different avenues and toward various potential consequences. The ability to define, judge, and balance what needs to be done, *who* will do *what, when* it will be done, *how* it will be done, and *why* it needs to be done, is fundamental. As a police officer, you will recognize this as basic police patrol tactics 101. You need to understand and balance everything around you. These principles are true in the business world as well: you need to know what the issue is and who the players are. For any kind of tactical crisis decision making, you need to be able to judge and balance a wide array of facts and opinions in order to develop a strategy for resolving the situation.

2. Understand the relevant facts, environment, players, and consequences.

Once you have defined the relevant facts—who, what, when, how, and why—you need to understand the environment in which you are operating, who the key players are, and how all of it affects the situation. It is equally important to understand what the potential consequences of your decisions and actions will be, both positive and negative. Who will be affected by each decision and how will it affect them? Are you in a completely private or enclosed environment or out in public where actions will have broader consequences? Concerns over consequences or who is watching should not affect your resolve to act, but it should affect how you plan. Do you need to be concerned about bystanders in the perimeter and danger zone? The success of an operation starts with good situational awareness and strategic planning.

It is vital to understand that everything is interrelated. You have to think through what your best case is, what your worst case is, and what can fall in between, so you can gain perspective on the whole landscape you have to work with and be ready for whatever happens.

3. Visualize the desired end result.

This is the single most important element, not only in crisis situations, but also for achieving success in any endeavor: visualizing what you want to accomplish. This is especially vital in high-stress tactical crisis decision making. Whether it is in business or police tactical operations, you need to know exactly where you want to end up and be able to visualize yourself at that position. You need to know what the end is before you can decide where the beginning should be. Only by knowing where you want to go can you design your plan to get there. Otherwise you will flounder, searching for an undefined end, and your mission will fail.

In high-stress situations, things come at you unexpectedly from every direction. It is very easy to become distracted from your mission. If something pushes you to the right, it is easy to move right; if something pushes you to the left, it is easy to move left. Although you may still be pushed, if you can visualize where you need to end up, you will be able to put yourself back on track, heading exactly in the direction you want. The discipline of visualizing exactly where you want to end up will ensure that even if you do not get to the exact place you wanted to be at, you will definitely be in the general territory; you will achieve your mission. Visualizing the end result is essential to keeping yourself from getting sidetracked and losing your focus due to distractions like screaming, breaking glass, gunfire, explosions, or any other unexpected events.

4. Communicate your desired end result and decisions.
Resolving any kind of major crisis or problem is never a one-person operation; it is always a team approach. As

such, you need to be able to communicate exactly what you are after. You need to express clearly why and how you are making decisions; only then will people know what to do and where to go. People truly do follow the leader, and in any situation, the leader has a huge influence on the culture of the organization, the team, and success of the mission. In both short-term and longer-term crises, it is vital to effectively communicate the desired end result and to make decisions with transparency and consistency.

5. *Inspire confidence; you need to lead!*

As a leader, you have to inspire confidence in your team. People need to believe in what they are doing. It cannot just be a job to them; they have to have a passion for the work. That is the only way to get past the inevitable obstacles that will get in your way. It is never just a simple beeline from A to B, with nothing in between. Only through inspiration and passion can those difficult obstacles be overcome. People need to be part of the team. They need to excel and they need to be recognized for the contributions they make. In order for everyone to be *all in*, people need a leader they can really believe in and trust.

So how do you apply these five crisis decision making principles in a disciplined, organized, and effective way? By following the tactical DECIDE model.

Sheriff's Chicago Violence Reduction Mission Strategy to Raise Quality of Life.

To Combat Extreme Violence in Chicago, the Sheriff Assigned Me to Lead a Mission to Create a New Model of Policing to Effect Change.

3-Pillar Framework for Reducing Violence and High Crime Communities:

I. Surge Enforcement; II. Community Engagement and Empowerment;

III. Community-based Programming

The Tactical DECIDE Model

THE TACTICAL DECIDE MODEL CONSISTS OF SIX key elements. It is simple yet effective and will equip you to make wise, consistent decisions resulting in a successful crisis resolution and mission success:

- Define the final objective and end result;
- Evaluate the ever-changing facts and circumstances;
- Communicate your final objective and plan;
- Inspire confidence;
- Don't hesitate or second-guess your decisions; and
- Execute!

Each of these elements is an express action that you must take as a leader. Change does not happen on its own; you make it happen. You are responsible for your decisions, actions, and the results. Do not let others or outside factors sway or control you. Although external factors and influences will change the dynamics of the situation, they should not control your actions. Tactical crisis decision making, done correctly, will lead to the desired end result.

Define the Final Objective and the End Result

Defining the final objective of a mission means that you are able to visualize the end state and clearly articulate your objectives. When making decisions along the way, do not lose sight of the desired end result.

If you do not know where you want to go,
you will never get there!

Even if you feel there is absolutely no time to strategize, there needs to be a clearly defined final objective. If you arrive on the scene of an active crisis where shots are being fired, the final objective could be as simple as halting the shooting and safely getting everyone out of harm's way. Of course, if you have time to plan ahead, you should develop something more structured and devise a full operations plan. However, life does not always allow for the luxury of time, and that is why it is important to be able to visualize and communicate the final objective; this is what you state at the end of an operation as "mission accomplished!"

As with anything, a plan is only helpful when people are familiar with it and can commit it to memory and translate it into action. Therefore, the final objective needs to be clearly articulated and simple. It should also be measurable, so that performance can be assessed. The point is to be able to personally visualize the end result and then communicate it to those involved so that they can also visualize it. The objective and the plan have to be defined in such a way that they resonate with the entire team. More than just an *idea*, it must be a clear objective the entire team can understand and passionately embrace.

Depending on the proficiency of the team, the objective and plan can either be intricate or incredibly simple. I am a huge fan of a very simple, big-picture final objective. Even the least prepared team member must be able to understand his or her role; if just one person does not know what you want done, things can become dangerously confusing.

Missions are dynamic, but the final objective has to be simply defined and fairly static—even though circumstances will likely change during the course of the crisis. There will be many times when unexpected changes occur during a crisis, and you may want to drop everything and deal with whatever they are, but this is not always the right thing to do. Staying focused on the desired end result is critical. This will help to ensure that you avoid panic or loss of direction. It means that you must know your needs, resources, and directives to get the job done. Of course, you can base your decisions on changing circumstances and external factors as necessary, but you cannot just make things up as you go; you need a big-picture final objective to guide you and your team.

While you must set a final objective, you must also set goals along the way and overcome challenges as they arise. Going back to my experience in Russia, my goal was to provide exceptional service to our customers in order to outperform our competition. After the initial incident with the group of men who came to our offices to intimidate us, I was surprised by the reaction of my visibly terrified VP. While my end goal remained the same for the business, I had to set the immediate objective of providing the assurance of security to the staff and ensuring that they were able to operate without fear.

> While you must set a final objective, you must also set goals along the way and overcome challenges as they arise.

It was important that I understood that the immediate issue was something to deal with, but it did not define our business or our end goal. I also ensured that the staff did not lose focus on our main objective, which was to provide service to our customers.

I first worked to relieve the fear my staff was feeling by hiring security personnel to guard the office. In reality, this was more about providing psychological comfort to staff than providing real physical security, but it was an important step to take. Though the issue caused fear and concern for the staff, we could not let it get in the way of working toward our original objective.

Immediate issues have to be dealt with, but they cannot consume and overtake your focus. In a crisis situation, you need to know what the end goal is. If it is a hostage situation, it is to release the hostages and get them out safely with as little harm to anyone as possible. Still, along the way, there will be distractions. An example is that as you are approaching a building to take action, suddenly shots are fired off to one side of the building. You have to make sure that you engage that immediate situation, while also ensuring that you do not deter from the original objective. In other words, you have to deal with the shots fired, but keep moving forward to rescue the hostage.

After working to eliminate fear among my staff members in Russia, my next goal was to neutralize the situation, which meant having to learn all about it. Neither my partner nor I had ever really faced this this kind of intimidation attempt before, so we had to understand everything around it, look for solutions, and determine what resources were needed to help resolve this issue. While we had to make these decisions immediately, we never deviated from our end goal.

Evaluate the Changing Facts and Circumstances

Circumstances can and will change quickly in the midst of a crisis or a mission. Therefore, you need to constantly evaluate and reevaluate the situation and adjust your tactics accordingly. You must ensure that you are working toward achieving the desired final objective.

Always be ahead of the situation,
not behind it.

In law enforcement, every tactical police officer and SWAT operator knows of a model called the OODA loop. The OODA loop was created by military strategist and United States Air Force Colonel John Boyd, who served in the Korean War and the Vietnam War. OODA stands for "Observe, Orient, Decide, and Act"—a successful model that has been widely adopted by the tactical community.

Evaluating the changing facts and circumstances is very similar to the Observe and Orient elements of the OODA loop. In a situation in which things are constantly moving, you need to be able to evaluate conditions and understand how a change affects what you are going to do next. The reality is that there will be disruptions; things are going to be different from what you had planned for and you are going to have to make improvised decisions. Sometimes these decisions can mean making changes to your entire plan.

One tactical leader I respect calls reactive actions during the course of an operation, "Initiative-Based Tactics." I like his terminology because, inevitably, you and your team will have to make decisions as you go. However, the degree to which you can modify your plan will depend on your team's level of sophistication and training, and on the circumstances of the crisis; it is not one size fits all. The most important thing is to not allow change to negatively affect the defined end objective. The unexpected may push you to the left or the right, and that is fine as long as you do not lose sight of the true direction. You need to stay focused on that visualized end result.

There are situations in which changing facts or circumstances may also change the objective. Ideally, you will never shift your objective, but you cannot be completely closed to necessary adjustments. This is where your judgment as a leader is most important. It is a matter of knowing the key concerns, considering your people, and trusting your experience and instinct. When unforeseen changes occur, you have to decide whether or not to change your final objective in order to get the job done.

In my experience in Russia, my goal was to continue building a successful business. As the urgent situation arose, I worked to normalize the feeling among staff, then immediately sought to talk to experts who had previously dealt with this type of intimidation. The people I turned to gave me practical advice and also became my negotiators, as I did not know the language and was inexperienced in such situations. What I had not foreseen was that this would then create an entirely new issue that I needed to deal with. The people I turned to wanted to take over my distribution for the entire city, which was neither part of the bargain nor what I had expected. What had seemed like a solution at first, turned out to be a mistake and a whole new problem. Still, I maintained focus on my end objective and continued to neutralize the situation with an altered short-term plan.

There will always be unexpected developments and crises, but you must maintain focus on your end goal while constantly strategizing your approach. The most effective way to avoid the need to change the plan is to keep your objective simple. The power of a simple objective is this: the more straightforward it is, the lower the likelihood that you will need to change it.

This held true throughout this episode. At every point, I had two choices: to fight or to give in. My objective was to build a high quality mobile network to serve our customers; we were determined to democratize communications, so I analyzed the changing facts and circumstances and decided that giving in was not an option, for I could not serve my customers if I did not control my distribution or my company. Giving in would have limited the future of the business, and that was completely obvious to me at the time. If we gave in, we would never be able to run and develop the business independently.

While it is often not the intuitive choice, you must never let yourself be distracted by present circumstances, which can cause you to lose sight of the big picture. If I had been focused on the short term, I would simply have signed an exclusive citywide distribution agreement—and then just trusted that they would be satisfied with that arrangement. But I was absolutely convinced that in the long-term, such an agreement would not be good or right; therefore, I gave up the easy short-term solution to make sure that I maintained the long-term potential and my desired end result.

Communicate Your Objective and Plan

Dealing with a crisis is never a one-person job. Communicating your objective and plan and making sure that every team member clearly understands this objective and plan is critical. It is the key to success.

> A team is only as good as the leader's ability
> to communicate the final objective and plan.

Being able to ensure that your whole team understands what you want to accomplish and how you are going to go about it is absolutely fundamental. When you are part of a large operation, however, you will only be able to communicate the objective and plan to a few people, who will then have to push it down the line to their team members.

Therefore, the objective and plan should be easy enough to be articulated in a few very clear words. If the objective and plan are too complex, passing along the message turns into a game of Telephone; this means that by the time it reaches the last person, the message is entirely different. You need to be able to explain your final objective and plan in such a way that everyone is on the same page.

Successful crisis resolution requires every team member to understand the end result and his or her individual role in achieving it without a second explanation. Even when you are only at stage one of defining the objectives and creating a plan, it is important to keep things simple so that the objectives do not get lost in translation.

In planned tactical operations, you will have a written operations plan in which you assign team leadership roles, assign tasks, determine movements and positioning, delegate responsibility for intelligence scouting, map communications with outside agencies, specify tactical command, set sniper positioning, and define life safety and extraction plans, etc. When time permits, all these details should be written down in an operations plan. However, you do not always have the luxury of such preplanning, which is why your final objective and plan must be simple enough to be communicated quickly and effectively in the field.

Strong communication involves making sure that in a crisis situation there is a clear one-way channel of communication. There is a time for two-way communication, particularly in the planning stages. In large crisis management situations you will always have a large team and you will need input from various experts. When creating a plan and defining your objectives, input from specialists is absolutely vital. But when it comes time to execute, there can only be a sole decision maker, one team leader who is closest to the action and who has a defined plan and the full authority to execute it.

Inspire Confidence

Inspiration is extremely important when trying to get maximum efficiency and performance out of a team. The group needs to feel confident in its leader. Each member needs to trust your guidance, moving forward without hesitation. Your conviction and confidence will bond the team members together. Even more important, team confidence will increase team performance.

Inspiring confidence is critical because we humans are emotional beings. All members of your team are available for action; it is their job. But they will work better when engaged on a deeper level. People want to believe in something and they want to be led; they need a leader. As a leader, you must empathetically focus this basic human quality to the advantage of the mission. You achieve maximum effectiveness not when people are just doing their job, but when they really believe in what they are doing and want to make a difference. It is therefore your duty as the leader of the team to make them believe in you and in the mission. Inspiration may sound soft, but without it, you are not going to get the maximum results you require.

It is normal for people to hold on to a habit—to the thing they have done over and over. It takes inspiration and motivation to make people abandon their habits and improve upon the mediocre results they have achieved with them. Encouraging the team to internalize your defined final objective and implement your plan is vital if you are going to tackle a major operation or crisis since, by definition, such situations are not commonplace. Without the motivation, your team will not be able to accomplish a seemingly impossible task. You want them to believe in your cause, to be excited, to make a difference, and to take part in something greater than their own self-interest.

Leadership and inspiration are absolutely fundamental to getting your team through difficult, daunting situations. No matter the amount of training and field experience a team member may have, there will always be an element of fear involved in any harrowing crisis or potentially dangerous operation. That fear is generally very healthy. Your team's sense of fear can be very important and inspirational when it is managed correctly. A good tactical leader knows how to use the team's fear as an advantage—a stimulating influence. The pounding of one's heart and the rush of adrenaline bring urgency and inspire immediate action.

> Inspiration is an emotion that will allow
> the entire team to perform at its best. It is a
> force that can propel your team above and
> beyond the possible when necessary.
> It gives each team member a significant
> and meaningful purpose.

As I mentioned previously, while dealing with the situation in Russia, we segregated the crisis and let people at the company know that things were okay and that experts were dealing with it. This enabled the rest of us to focus on our end goal. To ensure that the people were inspired and motivated despite the issue at hand, we made sure that we were delivering results. This goes back to not losing sight of the end goal. We continued to deliver results and we made it a point to celebrate our results together in order to reinforce the excitement and show our confidence.

The VP, who had been visibly terrified by the initial encounter, was then leading the efforts to neutralize the situation, so it was important that he had the confidence of the taskforce and staff. To inspire this confidence, he never again exposed his fear to anyone. There were only about three people who saw his immediate reaction, but from that point forward, he made sure never to show any doubt or concern again. He went about it as methodically and firmly as he was able. It was extremely important for the team that he showed that self-assurance and strength. These actions allowed the company to move toward our main goal with confidence.

Don't Hesitate or Second-Guess Your Decisions

This is an extremely important element in the success of the DECIDE model: never doubt yourself or your decisions. In a crisis, whether it is a business fiasco or a police operation that takes an unexpected turn, hesitation and scattered thinking can destroy the confidence and unity of the team. Doubt and indecisiveness can potentially decrease the team's efficiency and exponentially diminish the likelihood of success.

From a leadership point of view, the foundations of a good decision are your judgment and experience. Raw facts and circumstances should never define your objective or guide your decisions. It is the application of your judgment to those facts and circumstances that must guide your decisions. You may find yourself in a situation in which the constantly changing facts and circumstances lead you to believe that you should be doing things differently. As any tactical leader knows, sometimes your plan needs to evolve and adapt to account for these changes. Making that shift, however, is easier said than done; you must be very careful about when and how you make it, so as to ensure that it is not misinterpreted as indecision. If your change in direction or tactic is seen as self-doubt or anxiety, you will lose credibility. An unsure leader jeopardizes the confidence of the team and puts the success of an entire mission on the line.

Therefore, as strange as it may sound, it is sometimes better to continue with the original plan, even if it becomes less than optimal, for the sake of keeping the team focused on their objective and not confusing them with ever-changing strategies. The team relies on a clear channel of communication, and everyone must be working toward the same objective, with the same plan. If you lack the time or venue in which to pull back and explain the change, you risk confusion, frustration, and misinterpretation—all of which can lead to the failure of the operation.

Let me present you with a hypothetical model in an effort to solidify the point I am trying to make. You are leading an operation that involves a simple approach to a building when suddenly two unexpected gunmen appear and start firing. The solution could be as simple as falling back, securing the perimeter, and reassessing the plan. Obviously, the conditions of the situation have changed and you have to reevaluate your circumstances. If you are in a contained place where you can safely regroup and plan without danger, and you know the building is empty with no other people inside, you can make that call to regroup. However, if there are people in danger, you may not have that luxury. If, for example, you planned for one shooter and there are three, but there are people in the building who are at risk, then you have to keep moving forward and adapt as you go. It is not likely that you will have extra time to stop, regroup, and discuss modifications. You must proceed with the defined final objective in mind—with faith in your team, their training, and the original plan with which you began the operation. Making reactive changes to the final objective will not only cloud direction, it will also weaken resolve and confidence, which can lead to an undesired result.

No matter the magnitude of the change in a situation, if you cannot safely pull back, regroup, and clearly communicate the changes to the plan, especially when people's lives are in danger, then you have to stick to the original plan, counting on your judgment and making appropriate adjustments as the operation unfolds. Not every situation and contingency can be completely planned for, and not every plan is perfect, but that should not make you doubt your original plan.

> Never let raw facts, circumstances, or outside influences cloud your judgment and throw you off your defined objective.

Above all, you must maintain clarity of communication and uphold confidence.

Again, it comes down to judgment. Let your discernment guide you and know that success cannot be forced. Have faith in yourself and your team, and never lose sight of the final objective. It is not being stubborn; it is believing in yourself, your plan, and your team. It is being a true leader.

My experience in Russia is a great example of moving forward without second-guessing decisions. I was the one that made the decision to use the group who ended up trying to take advantage of us, despite the fact that I had thought that they would be our solution to the initial problem. It was my decision to refuse their deal and face the consequences, which included threats against my life.

Still, I never second-guessed these decisions. Instead, I kept moving toward our main goal, which was to build a leading global telecom company that was going to serve customers like no other. I did not let my decisions, which in hindsight were poor decisions, get in the way.

In the end, we achieved good results despite these poor decisions, and I am convinced it is because I did not second-guess myself. I never thought about this at the time, which is why I did not treat them as poor decisions. Had I second-guessed myself, there would have been a different result and there most definitely, despite my having communicated the end goal, would have been a lack of focus. If you are second-guessing, you are exposing yourself to a second or even third objective that will force you to reconsider your plans. This means that you are changing your goal, communicating inconsistently, and diminishing confidence. You will therefore be unable to meet the end goal. By never second-guessing, you minimize the likelihood of lack of focus and ensure that you are moving toward the end objective.

This is where strong leadership is fundamental to successfully reaching the end goal. Though I was not second-guessing, there were plenty of people around me who were. I ensured that all individuals moved toward the single goal instead of following their own agendas by having the judgment and leadership strength to refocus them and establishing that they could not have a stronger voice than mine in the final outcome.

Be sure to deal with and combat any competing agendas or plans in order to eliminate confusion and a lack of focus.

Execute!

The goal of the DECIDE model is to aid you in achieving a specific predefined end result: the end objective that defines the mission as a success.

A decision without purposeful and decisive execution is only a wish.

As tactical leaders and professionals, we are not in the business of wishes; we are in the business of positive results.

Things will always change as you go. Once you are in the middle of an active operation, changes can and will occur, and you will need to exercise your judgment regarding how best to deal with those changes. However, you cannot lose track of the fundamentals: making sure that people are fully inspired; that they have confidence in the leader, in the plan, and in the team; and that the adjustments made in the field are natural in the course of execution. Initiative-based tactics are fine, as are adjustments to your decision making and your frames of reference as the situation develops, so long as you keep yourself and your team focused and accountable to the end objective.

It is a matter, again, of strong leadership. You need the support of the people who have a significant voice on your team, and you need to earn your leadership through action and results, sharing of a vision; not just by the force of your command. In regard to my situation in Russia, though I had a leadership title, I was a twenty-five-year-old American, so I needed to build a team of allies to make sure that my decisions and approach were respected and implemented. You must build confidence and unity, but in order to accomplish this, you have to begin with recognizing your own limitations. You must also work with and around those limitations to execute the desired end result.

You must build confidence and unity, but in order to accomplish this, you have to begin with recognizing your own limitations.

Success always comes from a team; individual success is either short-lived or very limited because there is only so much you can do by yourself. When I went to Russia, I understood that I had no rights, that operating in Russia was a privilege, and that I had to earn the right to work in Russia through hard work and results. I also knew that I needed a partner and a team to succeed. If you are operating under the mind-set that it is a privilege, that you are there to serve people, you are much more likely to build a strong team and succeed in your mission. I needed to recognize that I could only serve the people of Russia by standing side by side with the people of Russia.

Similarly, in law enforcement, you cannot enter a situation pretending that you know everything and that everyone needs to learn from you. On the contrary, we learn from one another, and it is this understanding that enables all individuals to contribute what they have to offer toward meeting the end goal. I always understood that I was not an expert at anything. I was not an expert in the country, and, at twenty-five years old, I definitely was not an expert at business. However, I had a vision and I sought all the help I could and built the team. You define the mission and you give people the opportunity to contribute, and most people will exceed your expectations.

As I look through the history of VEON, against all odds, we did extraordinary things—and yet we were quite ordinary people doing them. Successful execution of a plan or tactic empowers each individual to do his or her part in getting the job done. At the execution level, it is about optimizing your thinking time and concentrating completely on the accomplishment of the defined end result.

The Virtuous Cycle of the DECIDE Model

The DECIDE model is a virtuous cycle of constant decisions that are all interrelated and vital to accomplishing the defined mission and achieving the desired end result. During execution, the final objective must always be kept front and center. You cannot and should not plan every single step in an operation ahead of time; rather, you must devise a strategy at the beginning and adapt and move forward as needed. As you execute your original strategy, you will have to go through your own mini DECIDE models; if this is done correctly, the model should empower you to make the best and most effective decisions, enabling you to accomplish the visualized goal no matter how dire the situation might be. This is true not just for the team leader, but also for every other member of the team.

It is not sufficient for only the team leader to understand the DECIDE model—all team members need to be able to comprehend it and use it at a moment's notice. In any tactical operation, whether you are clearing a building, pursuing an escaped criminal, or trying to rescue a hostage, there will be different stages of incident development. As a team member, sometimes you may be leading, while other times you may be following. Regardless of which you are doing, you need to fully understand your role and you must be passionately dedicated to the final objective. You must understand the importance of your position in the execution of the plan and always do your part, trusting and depending upon others to do their part at every stage and in every step.

Every team member must constantly be applying the DECIDE model, because although the situation and your role will be changing continuously, everyone needs to be working toward the same objective. The entire team will be going through the same virtuous cycle and you can therefore always count on everyone to be focused on that final objective and act to accomplish it, thereby ensuring that every team member has done everything possible to achieve mission success.

This DECIDE model does not come naturally, however. The only way to make sure that everyone is processing and going through the same DECIDE virtuous cycle is to train it!

Training to Implement the DECIDE Model

The DECIDE model is not only for a team leader or commander of a team; it is for all team members and all the participants in an operation to use. Therefore, everybody needs specific preparation and training on how to apply it correctly and effectively. It is meant to be a universal model, so that anyone—from a patrol officer to an emergency-management staff member—can quickly pick it up and use it if he or she is a first responder to a crisis, or part of a complex mission or operation.

It is an old adage in the tactical world that *you always perform up to the level of your training, rather than up to the level of your expectation*. Tactical proficiency comes from consistent training, after-action evaluation (accountability) and analytical chalk talks on the whiteboard. Training the DECIDE model is no different. You need to create scenarios designed to challenge your officers, operators, and supervisors to DECIDE. In your after-action briefings, you should do an in-depth review of the decisions that were made and the decisions that needed to be made. At the end of an exercise, ask the following questions:

- How did we do on our decision making?
- Did we do well?

- Where did our decision making fall apart?
- Did anyone lose confidence along the way?
- If so, what made you lose confidence?
- Did everybody understand the plan?
- Was it too complicated?
- What did we forget?
- Why did we keep going if we knew the circumstances were changing?
- What was behind that judgment?
- Did we achieve our final objective?

Having this kind of dialogue reinforces the fact that decision making is not just theory; it is a tool for successfully getting the job done.

In law enforcement, we have firearms training, tactical training, and even cultural and sensitivity training. This is an obvious need and everyone gets it. But there is very little training in leadership, organizational management, team management, incident management, and tactical crisis decision making. These topics are generally overlooked, so officers simply have to pick up knowledge in these areas along the way. People figure that if you are already in a leadership position, you should just go lead and get it done. Even in business, there

People figure that if you are already in a leadership position, you should just go lead and get it done.

is very little training; it is assumed that people in leadership positions know how to be leaders.

There are certain industries that are more geared toward this kind of training than others. The airline industry is one such example. Airlines are well known for instructing their senior leadership in how to deal with plane crash crises. When a crash occurs, reactions must be immediate and transparent. If the leadership gets it wrong, they will be seen as incompetent and the airline will be at risk of losing the confidence of the people it depends upon for future flights and revenue: its passengers. Because of this, if the airline industry spends a great deal of time on training and making sure that their teams are fully prepared to react immediately if a crisis were ever to occur.

Unfortunately, apart from the airline industry (and recently, the oil industry), there are very few industries that focus on that kind of training, and the law enforcement profession certainly is no exception. I strongly believe that this needs to change. There are many significant decisions involved in effectively handling a crisis. You need scenario-based training in which people can acquire hands-on learning and practice in tactical crisis decision making and leadership, particularly in complex crisis situations and under pressure.

Not everyone will be faced with the challenge of being in a leadership position during a crisis. However, if everyone is exposed to tactical crisis decision making training, then when the time comes that there is nobody else around but you—whether because the leader went down or any other reason—you will be prepared to step up and lead. You will know how to make the calls, communicate with the team, and react (or purposefully *not* react) to everything that is happening, while always keeping your focus on the final objective and visualized end result.

Training in tactical crisis decision making is extremely important, and the best way to train it is through scenario-based training, in which you walk people through crisis situations and force tactical crisis decision making. This can be accomplished both by tabletop exercises in a roll call room and by throwing challenges at people and forcing them to make decisions in the field. In truth, effective training in tactical crisis decision making should be a combination of the two. Your reactions to the crises you encounter and the decisions that need to be made in a tabletop training exercise can be completely different from how you will actually react and what you will decide in the field. Having the combination of both training environments is an extremely powerful advantage.

In a perfect world, training in tactical crisis decision making would happen at the same time as the so-called hard training, the physical and task-based training that all officers must undergo. Decision making is so integral

Decision making is so integral to the process of tactical crisis management and mission success that it should be incorporated into an agency's systematic training. It should not be taught only as a separate, unrelated course ("OK, now we are going to do a section on tactical crisis decision making"), but rather, it should be incorporated into your tactical and regular in-service training.

You should regard decision making as equally important as shooting, tactical entry, and self/buddy-aid training. Law enforcement agencies already implement training in areas that do not have nearly the same potential impact as decision making. In law enforcement, unfortunately, many departments and agencies are limited in the number of hours they can afford to train. At the end of the day, training time is money and it means taking officers off the street, paying overtime for training or to backfill officers on the street. Therefore, law enforcement agencies have to choose what is going to give them the most return on each dollar of investment in training—what will best prepare their officers to fulfill their mission to "protect and serve."

I argue that training in this kind of tactical crisis decision making would not only increase the success rate of missions and operations, but also increase an agency's overall supervision capabilities in day-to-day operations. The DECIDE model has many basic leadership and decision making principles and tools that can apply to a myriad of different situations. It is primarily focused on its application to tactical crisis decision making, but training in tactical crisis decision making will yield huge benefits in a variety of other areas.

Training officers to use the DECIDE model also shows the whole agency that the leadership believes that decision making is an important part of doing one's job. Knowing how to make decisions, understanding how decisions are made, and having the ability to employ tactical decision making practices are very empowering skills to possess. When the command staff recognizes the importance of tactical crisis decision making, the rest of the organization recognizes that decision making is an area on which they can and should focus in order to excel and advance.

The result of having the command staff and the field personnel completely aligned at all stages is incredibly powerful. It is not the norm, but if you, your field personnel, and your command staff all train together at the same time, and all have the same mind-set and the same tools, you will acquire a great deal of of power. Having unified tactics, training, and knowledge makes everything more streamlined and more effective. Empowering decision making among your officers will always help keep everyone focused on the communicated plan and final objective of a specific operation and/or the strategic objectives of your agency as a whole.

Lastly, it is important to train not just the body and the mind, but to also inspire and train the soul. Soul is the inner strength that drives you to want to make a difference. It is the extra push you need to surpass what you normally could have or would have done. It is what gives you that special strength, courage, focus, and inspiration to achieve and excel.

I truly hope that DECIDE has given you a practical tool and motivated you to want to apply, train and share this framework model and book with others. My aspiration is to see law enforcement agencies, tactical commanders, SWAT team leaders and operators, and police officers across the nation are as prepared as possible to lead, train and make the best possible tactical decisions in crisis situations.

Acknowledgements

IT IS ALWAYS IMPORTANT TO THANK THOSE whom you love. I have never taken my wife and boys for granted and they have always supported the sometimes-crazy things I do. They are a blessing and the inspiration for all that I do.

I have been very fortunate to have had many courageous leaders in law enforcement who were singularly focused on their passion to fulfill their mission. Chicago Alderman Chairman Ed Burke, Winthrop Harbor Police Chief Joel Brumlik, and Cook County Sheriff Tom Dart all dismissed the potential negative comments they might have attracted by giving me the chance to lead and prove myself in a field in which I was new and untested.

Throughout my continuous education in law enforcement, I have had an enviable list of mentors and believers, three of whom I would like to acknowledge: Winthrop Harbor Commander Dan Bitton, who has always encouraged and pushed me; Cook County Department of Homeland Security and Emergency Management Chief of Staff Ray Hamilton, a former Chicago Police Department lieutenant and a founding member of the Chicago SWAT High-Risk Entry Team; and Chief Eddie Burke, who taught me street smarts on the South and West sides of Chicago and was the first person to motivate me to get involved in law enforcement.

I praise God for always having led me on a path that has blessed me, protected me, and filled my every day with challenge and opportunity.